A mayo, [...]
support. I [...] you
enjoy this book and that you
feel blessed and cherished after
you read it ♡

FORCE OF NATURE

Keep lighting
up rooms with
your smile!

With Love,

FORCE
OF
NATURE

ODEMI E. PESSU

NEW DEGREE PRESS

FORCE OF NATURE

ISBN   978-1-63676-836-6   *Paperback*

978-1-63730-206-4   *Kindle Ebook*

978-1-63730-280-4   *Ebook*

*I dedicate this body of work to my mother, my
biggest cheerleader and favorite teacher.*

*And to my nieces, Christelle and Isabelle, who inspire
me to be a better woman with each new day.*

CONTENTS

AUTHOR'S NOTE

———

As a young girl, I was enamored by the stars. I would stay up reading, imagining myself as the characters in my favorite books, and looking up at the bright lights in Georgia's empty rural sky. I would sit and scribble my dreams into my favorite composition book, silently wishing that my life could be different—easier, fuller.

I saw my first shooting star a few months ago, while writing this book, and I was amazed by the gratitude that washed over me. I was grateful for the chance to begin again, the opportunity for rebirth. This time, I was secure in my divinity and power. How funny it was for me to finally see a star fall out of the sky just as I have finally realized all I've ever wanted is already mine.

I think of my fondness for nature and the beauty of the wilderness that surrounds us. Sparrows fly unwittingly; seasons ebb and flow in divine timing. Fires rage while flowers bloom and dandy shores welcome passionate sunsets promising something familiar, yet new. Nothing is controlled, but everything is connected. We can learn so much about ourselves by paying attention to the subtle lessons from Mother Earth. She shows us that every aspect of our beings contributes to the beautiful ecosystem that is our mind. With her guidance, I have learned to embrace the enigmatic parts of myself and bask in life's beautifully crafted chaos. Our Earth never begs for permission to exist; she shows us every day what it means to be free. Be it through tree stumps that join hands over time or the bright smile of the moon and her many phases, our Earth reminds us that it is okay to change, and it is okay to grow. But most importantly, it is our natural state to exist freely. That is when we thrive.

As such, it is a longstanding frustration of mine that African women globally are so often policed. Be it the way we wear our hair, or the way we choose to dress, or even the ways we mourn and cry or express our feelings, African women are often forced to shrink ourselves for the comfort of others. African women often lean into a narrative of self-sacrifice because that is what we are taught. We are taught to cater to the needs of our parents before our own; we are taught to uplift our husbands and our children even if it means burying ourselves prematurely. We are taught to view a life of second-class citizenship as one that is expected, not to be challenged. African women have built the backbones of society on the African continent, and it was our forced labor that catapulted Western societies to their supposed greatness. It is our wit and our wisdom that act as a sage and guide even outside of matriarchal structures. We are shoulders to cry on and bosoms to suck, but seldom are we given a listening ear. We are groomed to view happiness as a luxury, instead of our God-given right. But I am writing this lyrical manifesto as an ode to who we are in our entirety. We deserve happiness, and we deserve the freedom to define that happiness for ourselves.

I am blessed to have grown up in a household filled with proud Nigerian women who taught me the value of tenacity and to take up space without chipping away at my own value. The steady flow of their love nourished my dreams and transformed my secret streams of consciousness into waves of action. I was precocious, enthralled by the idea of becoming someone who important people listened to. My parents did not raise me to view my Blackness as a hindrance; they did not tell me that my femininity was something that would derail me on this path to greatness. No, they told me I was brilliant. They told me I was special. They told me I could be anything and everything I wanted in this life as long as I have faith in God. I believed them; how could I not? This self-assuredness manifested itself intensely during my teen years. I wanted so desperately to show my parents that their unwavering belief in me was not in vain. I wanted them to know that I was, indeed, brilliant and special. I tried so hard to prove myself worthy of achieving my aspirations.

Now, as I reflect on the prowess embedded in my Itsekiri and Ijaw lineage, how could I ever doubt that greatness lived in me?

My mother, my older sister, my aunties, and my older cousins are all Nigerian women who have shown me what it means to know my truth and what it means to advocate for myself when faced with adversity. My mother never ceases to remind me and my sisters that we are all uniquely crafted by God. During her infamous talks that still persist even in my "big age," my mother would point to her hands and ask us to assess our five fingers. Upon doing so, she would ask us to think about what would happen if one of the fingers should disappear. Then, she would transition to her closing point: all fingers are different, but these differences are needed to make the hand feel whole. Maybe some are short and stubby, or maybe one finger has a chipped nail that never seems to cooperate. Regardless of what set the fingers apart, my mother would use this analogy to show us that our individuality is what makes us special. I always think back to this lesson when I question my own unique attributes. It reminds me to know that my existence is important and that I matter simply because I am who I am.

However, owning this truth has not been a walk in the park. It has been a restless tornado, spinning me through not only bouts of trauma and sadness, but also joy and triumph. I left home at seventeen and journeyed in search of a place where I could truly shine. In some ways, I think I was searching for an external sense of the belonging and celebration I felt in the safe spaces I created in my mind. I was chasing something that I struggled to define, a sense of fulfillment that seemed to evade me the more I sought after it. In turn, I ran to the ivory towers of Brown University and corporate America. I learned about my history and what it means for a woman to decolonize her mind in the face of racism and discrimination. I learned about the power of respecting my past so I could welcome a brighter future. I lived in Amsterdam and learned the true meaning of community across borders as I formed new bonds with sisters who knew my soul before our faces could meet. I waitressed at a strip club during my master's program at an Ivy League university and learned that life is not black and white, and it is not my duty to make anyone comfortable with the colors I chose to paint my own canvas. I reckoned with childhood trauma and began to map out ways to escape the intergenerational labyrinths of pain so I could cultivate gardens of new hope and healing. I found my agency in the freedom to choose who I could become and to learn the lessons I was intended to learn, perhaps so I could share them with others.

Much like the seasons that God intends, my own story has come full circle. I have risen from the ashes, emboldened to continue my fight. I have grown from grounds of discontent into soft petals carried by serendipitous winds. The poems in this body of work were not written all at once; they are snippets and snapshots of different phases in my life. They are pieces of my heart, bare and open for the world to see, on my own terms. I held on to my words for so long because I was scared of what people would say, what they would think. Yet, as quarantine brought me to a still place—and, coincidentally, when I began taking this book writing endeavor seriously—I noticed a shift in my energy. I was back home surrounded by trees and surrounded by love. I was looking to God for answers about anything and everything because I was forced to make time to actually listen to the answers that came.

As I took time to listen to the soft whispers of the universe, my epiphany came.

The reason our souls find solace in the wilderness, the reason Jesus went to the mountain to pray, and the reason the land blesses us with food and nourishment when we harvest her with kind hands is because when we truly pause to see ourselves as clay—beautifully molded with love by God—that is when we walk in our power. And when I stopped being ashamed and afraid of the visions, words, and artistry that God shared with me in my quiet time, my soul levitated.

I felt like I had walked right into the eye of the tornado, forced to observe everything swirling around me. I was forced to feel it all—the isolation, the longings for freedom, the frustrations with the oppression and silencing of Black women in public and intimate realms. Ultimately, I was forced to be patient with myself, to realize there is no rush and there is no perfect finish line to cross. I had to find comfort in showing myself unparalleled compassion and trust that I would reconcile my emotions in due time.

As you read *Force of Nature*, please know that in the eye of the storm, you are strength. In your scariest moments of vulnerability, where you are worried your words will fail you, start with a whisper and don't be surprised when it becomes a roar. I hope my poems serve as a manifesto, an ode to our juxtaposed existences. We are the softness of clouds and the harsh pinches of lightning. The old soul of a willow's bark, and the blinding beauty of the sun. Teardrops of tired clouds, and the stillness of calm seas. We are so much and have even more to offer.

But I think it's time we do it on our own terms.

This is my love letter to who we are and all that we have the power to become. It is my hope that you will see your own truth reflected in my words. I hope glimpses of my story will empower you to write your own and take your life by storm.

I hope you find the courage to be open to love and its pitfalls, and to be open to learning from the stories of your elders and even those who view the world through rosy lenses of youth. I pray you look in the mirror after reading this book and recognize yourself for who you truly are. May your love for yourself blossom like sunflowers in a wild field. For they, too, look to the light for strength.

And, one last thing.

May you never forget the immense force of nature you are.

With love and light,

Odemi E. Pessu

WATER

---

that which nourishes us

Life begins with water.
It is the bare necessity of the existence we know.
In the rivers and seas that connect us to one another,
we are able to explore the deepest depths of our soul,
as a collective body and as individual droplets.
Water embodies the flow of that which comes naturally to
us—love.
We need water to survive, just as we need love
in order to live.

through uncharted waters

each beat of your heart
and tremble of your skin
whispers a song
a melody so sweet
a tune of happiness
when our bodies greet

the pools of your eyes
illuminated in the light
ask me a question
I do not ask
"why?"

tranquil, you lead me
through torrid pools
that sear with desire
I wade in your merciless waters
yet long to be subdued

breathe me in.
hold me.
caress me in your arms.

kiss me through the night
as waves ricochet between iron gates
your lips tell me stories
and I trace a path with mine

down to deeper depths
through Neptune's cage
and Venus' breast
I welcome you to my waters

giving you permission to
unearth uncharted seas
when our bodies meet

inhale me.

lover's bloom

If I'm a siren
You're a hurricane
Vivid in all your splendor
Engulfing my heart
in electric surges
and rushes
from the heart of earth herself

I'm not afraid
Dancing in your winds
I can't explain the sensation you bring
it tickles my cheeks like hydrangeas
on the roadside waiting to be kissed
I stop to relish
Enroute to your lips, I stain a violet hue

When moonlight races
across my windowpane
And sun rays fall
into feathered pillows

Our bodies still lay
Our hearts content

Your caress bounds me tightly
In the aura of your delight
For this feeling
I thank God above

I am blessed to call you mine

the first time with you

november first
brought fumbled limbs
intertwined
the hesitance of a fairytale kiss
sweet and new

i explored you
and you me

racing hearts and pounding lungs
caught me by surprise
you were unexpected
just like most things in life

i shared a part of myself with you
i placed it in your hands
i carved it in your skin
as if you were my man

what does that make you now?
a muse?
 a lover?

the subject of my dreams.

i hope not a fleeting glimpse
of temporary ecstasy
the curves you follow
the path of your lips
the pictures you paint
with your tongue's subtle flicks

take and transport me
to a place and a time
where nothing even matters
and you'll always be mine

college sweethearts

Friendship is the flutter of our lashes as we ride our bikes through campus, the illuminated summer porches of College Hill guiding our paths down winding streets and cobblestone sidewalks. It is the hidden snickers we steal in the back of the lecture hall, all the while planning our frappuccino date for right after class is over. It is midnight picnics on the Main Green because we are high and young and infinite, and this moment will never find us again. It is sitting on the fire escape and counting the stars and knowing that we are blessed to exist in this time and space.

Together with each other.

Loved and happy.

Friends.

Inamorato

I like it when you
look at me
like the reflection of the moon
in an anxious sea
you warm my skin
like soft candle flames
in the autumn night

I like it when you take
too long to say goodbye, lingering
like the sun's last rays
of evening light
kissing me softly
like violet petals
sitting on lucent marble steps

I tremble with joy
at your touch
and bathe in the brilliance
of your shooting stars
that shine

I like your heart
and the way it makes
mine

smile

Just You and Me

music can play while we watch the day
gradually become a memory we've made

the notes of your lover's drum, labored breaths
gallop through my mind
and I tuck them away
where they belong
folded in my heart
cosmic proportions
of your lips, subtle songs

stars will dance and the lights will sway
in moon's soft shine
as I sit there soaking in
your amorous monsoon
knowing that you're all mine

you can accompany me
on the journey to tomorrow
the beginning of our great perhaps
our hearts can weave together
baskets that carry words unsaid
across fallen tree stumps
linking chains that fell to rust
in anticipation of the sun's bright glow

we'll emerge into another day
reminiscent of what has been
but eager to meet the happiness
we'll be

all alone
just you
and me

sweet & early morn

Destiny's kisses
promise me forever
and Twilight's mist
signals a new beginning

therein I am   wandering

not lost
but still.
        floating between

                fleeting lucid thoughts

I am grounded all the same
in the deep roots of fervent faith
and the forgiving arms
that pull me up from last night's ashes
to come face to face with my reflection
and fold into love's sweet embrace

In the lambent light of a new morning
as I shift my gaze to adjust,

I welcome forever's promise
I welcome Destiny's kiss

love's terrain

love will not hurt me
it will free me

and my wings, clipped once before
will soar along the waters
those incessant waves
that guide your gaze to look my way

and the breath I feel within me,
within me, pouring out
will caress your broken bones

yes, my love
healing can coexist with ache

    like outstretched branches
that twist with the wind's pull

in the early morn
the twinkle of dawn's light
I pray your hands meander slowly
and find their way to mine
then again downwards, too
a firmer grip
my right thigh

holding me along a journey
one of discovery
a wandering heart's delight
into the wilderness
deeper still to go
towards unknown terrains of affection

an affection still betrothed

a gem of a dream

together they are one single gem
fusing the fragments of the earth
forest green leaves with mahogany streaks
that create the bark
in a rigid texture that becomes
hungry soil

ambient hues of light lilacs
and potent violets
stream the canvas
melting in with soft indigos
and pale pinks of late summer's petal

a golden dandelion unfolds into the air
to become the twilight
of a restful evening sky

powder blue splashes freely
into the sand of white
unconquered seas
rushed with greetings
segments of rain
deep aquamarine

one single gem
paintbrush in hand
swirling in motion
a wistful renaissance dream

Take Me to Church

Enshrined in the communion
of wandering thoughts
I move in rhythm with your being
The feeling of bliss I've come to know
as your lips minister to me

In your eyes I see the face of God
so in your oakwood pews
I surrender wholly

Giving you my love slowly
lose me within your sighs
and in the muffled glow of
New England's
starless night
I murmur hymns of delight
as you resurrect my body to new heights

When my breath finally catches
I'll hope you'll open your eyes
See the intricacies of this earthly body
what pleasure hides in my pews

crawl humbly to my altar
and let yourself be mine

make me whole

I imagine you
your blinding light
illuminating my irises
with the palpable glow
that comes from the joy of knowing
Knowing that I am yours
I close my eyes
and I am immediately engulfed
by the wave of emotion you alone can ignite

I peer through the window of your tabernacle
a glimpse at your Holy of Holies
Yearning to merely graze the edges of your glory
I run, panting
hungry in your direction
Following a trail of promises
that you alone can fulfill

With expectation and exasperation
I seek your face
I want your peace
to fill the crevices of my broken soul

I need you
more than I could ever begin to know
my feet falter at the steps of forever
the lookout of life's ominous cliff

to hold on to you
is the greatest testament of my strength
the meaning you bring to me
surpasses all understanding

and fills me up
where chasms grow
and ruptures widen
you appear in grand celestial wonder

you've come to make me whole
I need you
Lord

In the spirit world, women are Aje. . .The Aje rules us, rules the world, even when men assume that they have the edge.

My mother is Aje, and so are our sisters and wives.

—*FELA KUTI*

Welcome Home

When we come into this life, we have no idea what world, what reality, we will help to create. We have no clue how the universe will conspire to lead us across still waters to our greatest good. No. We enter crying, enraged by the change in atmosphere. The sudden coldness that awaits us beyond the warm encasement of our mother's womb. And then we grow and we stretch, fluctuating egos and evolving minds, into someone who dreams in technicolor. Who creates little droplets that water generations to come.

I have found the raging sea within me and I have seen her become still.
Prepared to conduct a journey of discovery
Receiving of the sun's gaze down on me.
I am warm again and Earth's womb welcomes me.
I am reborn
This time, conscious of what awaits me.

My manifestations are conversations with God,
momentary clouds that pass through.
Showing me pictures and shapes that only I can see.
The wind carries my whispered prayers to mother's belly.
Begging me to renew

so I am reborn
over and over
again.

In my revival I return to my roots.

Grandfather's guava tree and syrupy leaves shield me
from fire
when the sun is upset.
But the Warri sun never stays down for long.
Her phoenix rises each day.

Awake and brand new.
My footsteps in Mother's soil are washed away.

So, I walk to the Sapele sea and rinse my feet.
Baptized in awareness , so much so that when I look up
my eyes squint a bit, and my furrowed brows
give my confusion away,

I no longer feel lost.
Just surprised that I can see
a light that shines so brightly.
I am in awe that the sun does not smite me by day
And neither, I realize, has the moon by night.
So, I weep with great joy. And the salt water restores
my soul.
And I inhale this Holy communion
Through my Black body
So Brown and loved
So soft and true

My sorrows have drowned to the depths of the sea.
when I look down to the moving waters to kiss them
goodbye
All that reflects back is a blinding light

And I hear a voice.

Whispered prayers in the wind tug my hair.
And I look down to see, to my surprise once more

I am undressed
Laid bare before the Sapele sea
And the voice comes again.

It is Mother telling me:
 "Welcome Home"

THUNDER

---

that which shakes us

Thunder rumbles through the air without warning or regard.
It is the unexpected element of life that shake us to the core,
                    forcing us to reconsider what we believe,
                                who we are,
                        and who we hope to become.
We must feel our emotions,
feel the frustration let it roll through us,
fully and deeply,
in order to heal and welcome the sun
when she decides to return.

When Night Fell

even the night sky wept
as the stars returned back home
the valiant sun did little to numb
the remorse of a dusk now gone
daylight appeared in many shades
exposing all the truths
once concealed in the moon's dim lap
and shielded by night's cloth

run run run

my thoughts might combust
as my head spins achingly fast
my soul won't connect to my mind

I am watching the scene
but I've been elected to act
fallen curtains hold me captive
hopelessly anchored
to an outdated script

housed in a mausoleum
filled to the brim
with deceivingly beautiful lies

why can't I just do and be
what is it truly
who am I trying to be

I choke on my answer
to quell hushed tears
as blinding lights beat down my barricade

every day fades solemnly to grey

red curtains close, I can't build my home
not here on this solemn stage

> I want to run
> > I want to run (far)
> > I want to run
> > > I need to run (away)

heart made of glass

i thought i scared you away
when i told you all the bad things
but you listened

i fathomed how one could love
a being so broken
so shattered

yet you moved in close when the
jagged edges grazed your skin

how could you peer into the eye of the storm
unearthed by sinuous spectacles
glass floating in the air
whisked through the turbulence of my mind's might

emboldened with wonder, you continue
embracing the thrill of fatality

knowing the perils of exploration
but plunging in all the same

i still question how it is that
you can hear a symphony
when in truth I croaked
a requiem

reflection

I had a friend in grade school who hid her scars with a
black hoodie.
I wondered how often she allowed herself to be bare.
I wondered if she used the salt from her own tears to try
and heal the wounds only she could see.

the first time I cut myself, i could not feel the pain.
it's odd, how the smell of your own blood can elicit such
a response.
I wanted to feel anything, yet found myself feeling nothing
but the emptiness and loneliness I was trying so hard
to escape.

I hid mine the best I could.
Long sleeves, thick bracelets, silenced tears.
I hid the best way I knew how:
     In plain sight.
I felt invisible anyways, so it couldn't be that hard
to disguise something that no one knew existed.
     Looking back,
I wonder how things would have played out if i had a therapist.

I remember the envy I felt when, as an adult,
I read that Tina Knowles had sent Solange and Beyoncé to
therapy when they were younger.
Of all the things to covet in Beyoncé's life, that was it for me.
The freedom to explore pain, the invitation to understand
her own mind at such a young age.
The privilege of allowing herself to be bare.

I would have given the world to have that.

Nostalgia

as I made my way down the sidewalk
I found much needed asylum in raindrops
plummeting down

beating playdough drums
on the upturned whites of my palms

waves of nostalgia rippled through my mind
as I was reminded of the day

our buses departed
windshields stained

goodbye

Ribbon in the Sky for Your Love

Ribbons of your memory dance
through my mind
strings of gossamer
sometimes silk
frayed edges tickle me softly
sometimes suffocating
but always there

Love, unrequited, hangs in the air
and I wish I could listen to Stevie
and think longingly of your smile
I wish you were mine

not to have, but to hold
not to own, but to know

The last breath I took was the inhale
of your cologne
I wonder if you can sense
my infatuation
do you wear it on your skin
and tie it around your wrist

does it fuel your desire
to drift so far away

from me?

staircase to solitude

I cut the soles off my shoes
so I could walk lightly up the stairs
I became a vagabond of winding hallways
and sunken cedar floors
But when I reached out for you
you were no longer there

Through a winding ascension
and the diminishing flame of evening's hollow glow

    I followed

Blind, I became unable to see
I trusted you to lead me
more than I trusted the steps of my own feet
A hopeful crescendo came to a halt
as the floor crumbled in
and I felt myself
        fall

Aware too late
Destitute, I stumbled to my fate

and I beckoned for you
I cried

    for my heart to follow

yet
I could not breathe
my love
    my hope
        our dreams

sustained momentarily

        in the callous space that now exists between you
        and me

and I crippled slowly
into the carcass of a slain being

alone

alone

alone

september skies

every day feels the same
sometimes blues
but often greys

then the browns mix in with the beige
and tears fall
and the red in the streets stain
cold hands meet closed eyes

I watch this same scene repeat year after year
day after day
etched in the ripped fabric of a national cloth
stained with red and split at the seams

and I sit
and I breathe
and I choke
and I heave

then I rest and forget
but never truly
not fully

red pavement cracks beneath
blue chokeholds in the light
I'm still aware and enraged
at these damn september skies

filled with grey

Where Does the Black Woman Go?

Where does the Black woman go to dream
Where does she find the wind to let it carry her
Seated on clouds as fragile as the cotton picked
in grey Georgia fields

Where does the Black woman go to laugh
Is it in the arms of her auntiecousinsister
Lover?
Where does she soften and fold into the arms of
one who cares and longs to see her smile

Where does the Black woman go to live
Freely and unrestrained
No longer defined by syllabic chains
of the English language
A foreign tongue of slanted insults
drizzled down through time

Where does the Black woman go to be alone
Just to exist, nothing less and nothing more
To think and sigh into a large cup of ginger tea
And stretch her hands to the sky, feet planted
in earth's soil, no mosquito bites in sight

Just orange hues of dusk
And pink sunsets to match
The quiet hum of a heart churning
Under a half moon's light

Where does the Black woman go when the sun finally sets
after a laborious day's end

Where does the Black woman go?

Blossom, Dear

My back is swollen and my hair is wooly and my arms
fragile
as I cradle a future
tucked in abundant dreams
of an unconditional love supreme

I worry the flower I plant will shrivel
I worry the soil will choke her roots
I worry the sun will forget her face

But
    even still
        I cannot return home

I cannot continue to mince my words to make you feel free
I cannot continue to shield my existence to uplift your own
I cannot continue to labor and watch your trees bear
the fruit of my tears

So how do I continue to plant and water
for my future blossom
My future flower
How do I nurture you when my own pot is dry

I don't want to water your soil
With raindrops from my foggy eyes

Forced to Feel

I've formed a bad habit of holding back tears
Letting my reservoir over
flow
Until there is nothing to hold back the water
the frigid swells that carry hurt
and happiness
Or the vessels that float in between
those polar opposite ends of my being

And each time I let a tear go
It somehow feels
like an unbearable monsoon
The ripples through my body
a small island shaking in a summer storm

When my cheeks heat up, ears on fire
Heart leaping to escape this burning hell
I am reminded that earth weeps in small waves too
And fire screams its fears into a smoky ravine

When dormant volcanoes lament a lost life
Cracks are formed
the earth sees
Red

Sanguine sunsets greet me ahead
And my feelings float through an inevitable storm
where blood trickles through
alabaster fountains

As I bleed
So does the land

seaweed bridges
scarlet steps
Covering old battlefields again

For Anani

my heart feels the gravity of stones
tossed across infinite pools of cobalt blue

and the reflection of your heart
in the skies of my swollen eyes

my goodness, you are
still
love personified

and though your touch evades my grasp
and my heart
threatens to crumble

with each passing day

your words float within me
they comfort my soul

though this life is finite and fickle
my heart will forever know the warmth of your smiles
my spirit will endlessly toast to the man you are

as mortality rears itself
to the forefront of what seemed
unfathomable

I carry myself afloat
upon the clouds of hope you left within me
and as I levitate higher
further from the ground

I hear your angel voice calling
me to ascend

in remembrance of you

Thank you, Anani
Thank you

Have Mercy

Tears rolling down
thunder shakes my soul
Stifling the sound of heartbreak
I swear I could drown
to the pits of Earth's mantle

Understanding less each day
Looking for answers
In the unwinding scroll that binds
my past and my future into
one
I found myself subdued to new depths
broken

Torn at the seams
I begged for mercy
kneeling with my chin upturned
For you to shine down on me
I sought a strike of lightning
from heaven's gates
a sign you were there

When I could see what I wanted to see
I felt myself exhale
Flares from your prismic gaze touched
my head with your sharp edge

At last I could hold you
Down on my knees

At last I could hold you
Down on my knees

The Prayer

I am a well

Half empty
Down in the trenches
But still so close to the earth
She whispers to me at night
And births new beginnings each day

But when will my own cup runneth over?
When will a fortress of salvation surround my
forsaken heart?
When will love overtake the anguish that entrenches
my soul?

Surely goodness will
follow me

All the days of this life
So long yet so short
So fast yet so slow
filled to the brim
silent in slow rain's echo
But I am assured
by the lightning that strikes in the midnight hour
and the mountains that quake
when the morning rejoices

Surely goodness will
follow me

As I dwell in the house of the Lord
Earth's belly will not swallow me whole
Her womb will birth light
for my path
in the shadows that surround me
triumph finds my hand in the dark

I am well

When you disrupt womxn, you disrupt the ecosystem.
Keep violating our bodies and see what comes this way.

—IMA DIAWARA

Revelation

Soft pitter patter of the Georgia rain
reminds me of memory filled puddles
to drown out the pain
And if I listen closely
as I tend to do on misty mosquito-cloud days
I can hear choirs worship and repeat the refrain

Holy is He, Holy is He
Lord Almighty, Holy is He
But when I close my eyes to join in
my heart cries

Holy is she, Holy is she
until one aunty smacks my hand
and sneers
 "Will you hush! That is blasphemy!"

So then I sit still and pray that the wind
will carry me far far away
Three clicks of my heels and I'm there

Until my body stirs
and I wake up once more
Unmoved and unyielding
To find myself wading through flooded marshes
Savannah's molten terrain

The rain, however, has stopped
And wet foliage paints the concrete
blood red and guerilla green

As I inhale this view, still like a dream
My breath pauses to exhale a sweet
melodic tune

I am free indeed, free indeed
Holy is She, Holy is me

Again the wind howls
and abruptly I stop
Scared of the residual punishments to come
A whistle sounds again
First softly, then louder
To become a chaotic cacophony
of blasting horns and dancing trees

Are the end times near?

I quickly close my eyes and begin to pray
Dear God, please send me a sign
Or a feeble note to say
this freedom is mine

Once I look to the sky
Basking in the brazened bronze
of the sun's ardent light
Reckoning is near
and heaven's gates await

I see a sign
Red hues drizzle down
as I tread the winepress of fury
And in this moment I am radicalized
Ready to sing my song
Stomp my feet

Holy is She

Redemption is finally mine

FIRE

—

that which emboldens us

When life scorches us, we must bury the remains of our
old selves and trust
that our phoenixes will rise again from the charred
remains of what we left behind.
As we levitate from fallen embers, we must do so boldly
and without fear or apprehension of what is to come.
Revolution's inferno is an uncontainable wildfire,
setting souls ablaze
and igniting the desire to fight for what is right.
Let the warmth of your heart's fire radiate freely,
and welcome the change that happens when you do.

A Case for Mami Wata

I let the sea's cold hands embrace me
                and carry me forth

then back
      then forward again

I heard stories when I was younger
Of the queen of the sea
and how her evil highness would creep
in her sapphire gown
to steal the souls of men
who wanted to feel the iced tips
of her frozen limbs

She would devour them
imprisoning their hearts
with the promise of riches
and the curse of infertility in return

I see the parallels across time
these stories of yore
The lust of sirens
and jezebels on the hunt
Demeter's anger
but never her hurt
Eve's miscalculations
and her progeny's plight

So it leads me to wonder
how many stories did men write

about the wickedness of women
witches flying in the night
relentlessly in search of helpless men
to entrap in silk-lined beds
and deceitful seductresses
femme fatales that feast
in the golden shadows of dawn

And why is it that
centuries since
traversing space and time
many moons later these fables persist
Blindly guiding our future
Patriarchs of time hold on to these tales
of Medusa's entrapment
But never Hades' snare

If these stories are true
And kings and conquerors fell
    from glory
        to dis
           grace
into graves of poisonous wombs

Why did Mary birth light?

Why did Esther's cries reach the heavens
and thwart a massacre so vast
And why did Miriam's love flow freely
through Pharaoh's treacherous Nile
And why did Atlanta's arrows pierce through
the heart of havoc to summon peace

Once again

Why do Willows that weep in feminine lairs
still rise and break heaven's gates

I ponder this and think
of Eve's exploration as Adam's right hand

And I ask God this question

Why did you make woman
the fall of every man?

I am a woman

and a woman of Africa.

I am a daughter of Nigeria

and if she is in shame,

I shall stay and mourn with her

in shame.

—BUCHI EMECHETA

Keeping Score

Tears in my eyes
fall
and cut
like slashes through a captured fowl
feathers soft, blood still warm

I hear screams at night
and in the shadows of the early morn
They echo through the belly of thick air
the kind that seeps and haunts
and hides their crimes

I hear her scream

It is an abducted innocence
choking on the aroma of fear
It rises to clouds and the skyscrapers
from which
the oga at top looks down

When he closes his blinds the storm quickens pace
with her body's nectar
spilling
from the hollow gourd of the Lagos sky
The ground's green is turned
to the color of crimson palm wine

But like a headless fowl
the cuts on her neck are still ripe
wet with the unwanted kisses
and the burn of a devil's tongue

How can a corpse kiss back
when the deed has been done?

Fevered thrusts
back and forth
will always leave a mark
on a severed heart cut in half
Where is the national uproar
the lace of funeral white
Where are the masses of mourners
machetes ready
ablaze and alert, ready to take flight

Instead bitter leaves sway
and plan Oshun's revenge
Her river waters
leave fresh tally marks on the skin of
bruised cheeks and the scratches of inner thighs

Our bodies keep score
of every woman's plight

Is This Love?

Black love is beautiful, but it is also

captivity

If you share my pain, if you hold my hand,
if you fight for me, I'll give you
"nothing," he said
nothing at all

And that is supposedly
loyalty

As I learn through age,
society expects a different kind
That which binds a mule to his master
even after the master feeds himself first

Our communities expect servitude
even during droughts
when our reservoirs of love and capacities for nurture
are struck by plagues
cyclones of disaster
ignorance and misogynoir

I am starting to think it is stupidity they want

forget
    patience
forget
    a listening ear
forget
    a heart that is wise
forget
    a stable hand to hold

a heart to have
for better or for worse

sadly, for our men
a blind eye would suffice

to hell and back

Pain that I cannot disclose
Not for fear of judgement
But because I can't beg
I drink mediocre merlots
until nighttime feels warm
And then I wake up the next morning
and
I try again

I have been to the hilltops
Trekked up a treacherous mountain
Hanging on to stones that break me

I have seen the darkness

Held it close against my bosom
like a child I wean
In hopes that tomorrow I will awake
to find her ready to stand up
and walk towards the light

I have journeyed alone
Through wicked forests
Fighting the vines that choke
And feeding the birds that fly

I have come out victorious
Blood tooth and nail
I have come out whole
Prepared to rise strongly
I have come out the tenth circle

awakened

Eyes adjusting to the bright waves
Across the way I let Lethe lead
Pulling and tugging me
through caves of discontent
into tunnels of disillusion
nonetheless taking me

forward

To the other side

getting over

I'm learning how to love again
to not wince at the thought
of tearing apart the brigade I've built up
around my heart
and I understand now
my capacity for love cascades
like lava
without end or shame

my back no longer bears the iron cloak
my soul beams through austere clouds

the hurt stings
but I rest assured that I am capable
of entrusting my heart
in someone's hands
and, too, taking theirs in mine

and what a marvelous thing!

to love
levitating across evanescent clouds
leaping through lily-clad meadows

and to know that
I have been wronged
my heart broken
ripped off my sleeve
Yet it still beats so
with stiffened legs

It gets up to dance
and laugh and hug
singing sonnets and odes
and I'm happy to know

I am love

I am me

I am free

Emancipation Proclamation

Remember when black art meant revolution
Remember when black love and black unity broke down
      concrete bricks
         weighing heavy
            stealing the air
               we could not breathe

Remember when black rage burnt these institutions to the
ground
And dared them to try to rise again

I want to taste the rage of the scorned
I am not asking
I am not begging

     I am taking

I am creating
I am nourishing my soul
Plaiting the fields
Of those who came before me
My tears water the earth
From there my freedom rings

Red seas part when I lift my hands
to dial the sky

God has said let my people go
And free we shall be

Rivers Girl

In times of discontent, I come
to the fertile soils of conquered lands
dripping in liquid gold
And I ask

What does it mean for me to call captured pastures
home?

Can I find freedom as a sailor
conquering seas of my own
and finding solace in the icy opinions
of waters who know truths as much as they know lies
bearing witness to abduction
carrying love letters in bottles
that will never drown

I find refuge in the lethargic stretches
of cobalt waves dancing
towards a molten sunset
out of reach

Do they abide by the moon's wishes
Or do they meander without direction
in search of bare skin
just something warm
at last
to offset the winter's cold

I sit here
watching them scurry back
                    and forth
and I marvel at how the movement of the air
touches us differently
Indigo ripples become ardent tsunamis
while the hair on my neck
stands still

As I feel tender kisses
amidst imminent storms
I am at home in the wilderness
and relaxed by her chaotic unknown
As temperature changes forebode
a setting sun
I can't bring myself to leave
Even obscured by evening's shadow
my sailor heart beats on

Canoes no longer wait in the distance
to receive my prayers for protection
I shout my desires into earth's abyss
and hope she hears me
and hope she bothers to listen

The sea revels in resistance
she comes and goes just as she pleases
And perhaps
it is for this reason we are friends

Bound to an indignant existence
Contesting constraints of grainy shores
While washing away stubborn stones

I hear the cymbals clap with trepidation
in the cool breeze
of isolated coastlines

We string together gossamer wells
wistfully through the tendrils of our exposed hearts

I hear the cymbals clap in the cool breeze
of isolated coastlines
Now, with a fervor unseen before

But the sea and I have an understanding
I don't feel foreign in her waters
or frightened by her power
I'm inspired by her magnitude

It teaches me to know my own

birthright

I get carried away
with the weight of the world
I can't feel foot
Sunken in soil
I raise my wings overhead
Like an erstwhile healed fowl
sputtering blindly
through a deserted compound

It was black as the night
when I first tumbled forward
Black with no light
when I stretched my limbs outward

Towards eternity,
                    I walked the fields.

Gliding through high grass and fallen greens
I meandered through an Ancestor's grave
Buried beneath seaweed and locked with iron keys
I pay tribute to this legacy
A life hidden from me

This is my birthright

I am my grandfather's emancipated vision
Persevering through the whip
of hostile forayers
Raising a sword to headmaster's hand
I am the thoughts of chiefs conjured in the morning

Seated on thrones threaded with ivory
and sipping from glasses peppered with gold

Leaning against the bark of this regal lineage
emancipates my fears
Positioning me to stand tall in the face of adversity
history's hard truth
society's deceit

Without hesitation
I walk the land
once taken from me
I own the land
I reclaim my being

This is my birthright

10.20.2020

what does it take to be a martyr
assassinated for a cause
burned alive and subdued
by greed and pain

from the cracks of a barren soil
our cries seep out

in the hollow caves of consciousness
that our leaders seem to lack
the hands of history's goliaths
wring out
a blood filled bath

what does it take to fight
relentless in pursuit
of life's illusions
distant promises of humanity's grace

a bullet to the head?
a rope to the neck?
perhaps one last plea for mercy?

the land will not forget
the corpse of freedom is embedded
in the eye of an eagle shot down
from the sky

the seas that hold us will remember
as will those of us that sink quickly
into the sand of crimson shores

the red sea will part imminently
and ripple through the concrete
that weighs on our backs
overcoming the statues that stand guard
defending the capitol's prize

We are the salt of the revolution

We will never die

it holds on because it can

I want
to bleach your kisses
off my lips

then burn the imprint of your
fingers from my skin

I want to obliterate the shadow of your insults
to erase your calloused footsteps
from my mind's terrain

but still, I reminisce of sweet nothings
sang during our fugitive bliss
only at times when I've paused
afraid to begin again

today is a fresh chirping
I sing an unfamiliar song
I'm on a run now, racing forward
I'm halfway towards the sun

As I thaw broken shards
into fevered mercury pools

Please

Do not find my hand in the embers
if tomorrow I combust into charred remains
Do not collect my ashes
As if they are yours to own

I am growing something new
I am no longer the same

I was never yours to take

By Any Means Necessary

I hate that my thirst for the oppressor's blood to shed
may liken me
to that same barbaric picture they paint
of the Black woman.

Angry.

I am angry.
I hate it, but I know it.

I am enraged by what I see
strange fruit poisons my eyes
and stains my lips blue
Seething streets swallow me whole
and I wake up each day to brick towers
sitting on my chest

So yes, I am
mad.
But I refuse to   *run*
mad
because my mind is all that I own

Sanity grounds me in the soils I will inherit
in the trails I am yet to know
in the wealth I am yet to hold

I will escape Goliath's garden
Pharaoh will fall slain at my feet
The bodies of giants will break
and shatter through the ceilings
I once could never reach

Grasping the necks of fallen soldiers
knife in hand
my palms become red
with crushed cherries from fresh wounds

Guns ablaze I lift my eyes to the heavens
Am I a sinner for a longing to be free?

Or is it only wrong because I will take that freedom
Prayers on my lips
Bullets prepared to fly
Ear pressed to heaven's door

By any means necessary

SOIL

———

that which we grow from

We must cultivate our lives as we would a precious garden
and trust that we will blossom in divine time.
As our souls discover new terrains of emotion,
we find an unwavering hope for new beginnings.
This courage to believe in the propensity of our greatness
and the promise of love is what grounds us
even when the terrains we tread feel like barren quicksand.
We are harvesters of love and light.

Want

I want
the security of knowing the air I breathe
the life I live is not challenged
Critiqued by the devil's eye
subjected to the ominous gaze
the hold that is
not palpable

You must feel it—
you must feel it wash over your feet as they sink into
quicksand on the cusp of change

I want to feel the waves of liberty's river
rush between my toes
I must experience my heart's beat
I must feel it swell because
my world is restructuring itself before
my eyes

I want to feel my tears dry because my
mind no longer threatens to combust
under the weight of my worries
I want to feel my breath seep out calmly
under the moonlight
because my heart no longer quickens pace
from the fear of somber valleys

I want so badly this future that
teases me in the horizon
One where life's daily bread awaits me
and my feet float above scorched concrete
Where I walk,
       dance,
           and step
through meadows
planted with loving seeds

I want to walk
confidence in my hand

I want the goodness and mercy of tomorrow
to find me today

of *paradoxal* mind

my soul is a paradox
who sought the sun
when the moon smiled down
whose grains of hot sand
peppered my chilled seaweed crown

my mind is a metaphor
a raging lioness,
poignant and unyielding
seldom slowed by the stares
from evil eyes in the night

my heart is an untold sonnet
tender with the melodic pull
of a vivacious song
three part harmonies that carry me
through empty corridors
to find the concealed light
at the end

my body is an illusion
a statue of hidden dispositions
rigid yet faint
crumbling silently
where the years have taken a toll
yet standing upright, still
with a heart melted to stone

Redemption's Light

If soft hands can soon become calloused,
surely the residue of your fire's timber
roasting
can one day become a cool saline breeze
off the coast of Dakar
where rose waters welcome
blue lily heavens

As emerald greens can create rubies
in autumn's amber air
Surely golden hues can overtake a solemn sky
and beg it to shine again

 "Oh please, shine"

If hearts can know each other
and feign forgetfulness the next night
perhaps
I, too, can play tricks on my own mind

And I can beg my spirit to live and to find
her luminous light

 "Oh please, shine"

Even when she wants
nothing
nothing more
than to shrivel up and die

As branches mourn
fallen leaves
and winter's winds race on

Surely my heart's song
can quicken pace
and rejoice in the light
of spring's inevitable dawn

"Oh please, shine"

Praying for endless days with you

How do we fall in love
and quietly come to terms
with inevitable endings
and partial goodbyes
not all the way gone
but gone still the same
lingering in hollow doorways

How do we reconcile the remnants
of lost realities that taunt and teeter
from the ledge of hope
I tie myself to each night
praying for endless days with you

I pray that we can live and love
and be together
so I can hold your hand
interlacing lonely fingers
and eat off your plate
and help you when you need it
and hug you tight
buried in the warmth of your chest

Because I love you

Your voice echoes through my musings
Silently I curse the thought
of you leaving my side
the violent idea of an existence so mighty
evaporating

I cannot fathom your exit
I will not clap in the end
for the return of an angel

So I clasp my palms
and hold yours in mine

I pray for endless days with you

august interlude

country stars in the night
glistening through trident maple leaves
though hidden within my peripheral
all seem to shine
a bright light
sketching your silhouette
into my heart's pulsating canvas

summer breeze
whiffs of air
seasoned with the spice
of nutmeg's potent musk
and cold pine cologne
carry the aroma
of a love not easily forgotten
one I wish everyone could know

though my heart seeks refuge
the clouds paint a picture
a vivid memory
captivating the sun's attention
stalling her return
stealing her warmth

your smile
I see
appearing as the lone crescent of the moon

still,

the seasons quicken pace
filling me with hopeful anticipation
until I'm graced with the image of your face

once more
when we lay
beneath the country stars

longing for love in quarantine

I lay my head down each night
whisked away through an abyss of longing
A yearning that taunts me
like the lull of my favorite song's end

My anguish knows no bounds
as I long to feel the warm
yet tight
grip of a lover's hand around my own

To lift and glide with the
air of love, a summer's delight

When dusk welcomes my thoughts
ever so expectantly
My lucid imaginings enamor
my half-awake being

My heart's wishes are held
captive in the hushed breaths I inhale
and release into pink satin pillows

A cinematic dream for swollen eyes
    A rendezvous for a sunken heart
        An oasis for a desert mind

Finally, I drift off into a slumber
emotions still burning
in my heart's waning lantern
I am left only to feel

the tender kisses

of the
Georgia

night

sky

A Lover's Pipe Dream

If I had a love to aspire to
I would hope that terra-cotta waters
would fill your eyes each night
In the candle light of my heart's warm
incessant glow

If your hand somehow found my own
In the strange darkness that only we know
I pray fervently the night breeze
would sing us to sleep
and cast the flames of our frustrations
into eager kisses
between scorched lips
hot with the fire of requited compulsion

If only our love could burn like those flames
hungry for more
Oh, how intensely we could grow
I'd see my glow in your soul
and you'd see your heart's reflection
palpitate in sync with my own
Our somber limbs
would lay intertwined
where lucid thoughts ramble aimlessly, alone

And if we could just be
here
Perhaps eternity would no longer feel
like a peek into a lovely oblivion
obscured by the haze of grey mirrors

and opaque glass screens,
stained

My lungs would no longer choke
and cry out for the air only you give

If I could be yours, only,
my dear,

Would it still be
nothing more than
a lover's pipe dream?

Craving Crescents

At night I pray and crave your smile
If not today
Then in a little while

Why must I wait
and make no sound
like the quiet hush of summer days
under pinkberry clouds

Sitting here, I wonder

Does wilderness long to be calm?
To meander endlessly as a stream
While sister seas rage on?

And do the rings of Georgia oak stumps
carve out memories of yore
like the shape of your half-moon lips

On the crescent of my own?

love in the afternoon

afternoon cries
doused in pleasure
transform freely
morph slowly
into evening kisses
underneath sheets that keep me
wrung around your neck
like a ribbon tied too tight
or a branch scared to fall
into a rocky abyss

it shouldn't hurt
the fall should be soft
like a quiet drifting spiral
into yesterday's dreams
and today's fresh fallen leaves

explore, but do not claim
take, but do not own

be gentle with my heart
her wings are healing still

slowly
but freely
through evening kisses
with you

Time by itself means nothing, no matter how fast it moves,
unless we give it something to carry for us; something we value.
Because it is such a precious vehicle, is time.

—AMA ATA AIDOO

My Time (is mine)

I remember that scary plunge. I ran from what I could not
yet know

> Spiraling
> Floating
> Suffocating
> Pleading
> Wishing
> Waiting

Then leaving to seek more
Only to find myself
Repeating the same cycle of sensations
over and over

Feeling pain I cannot disclose
Not for fear of judgement
But because I fear no one will care
I drink until nighttime feels warm
And then I wake up the next morning
and
I try again
    and again
        over and over
            again
and again

Until I stopped to stare over the ledge
And ask myself what I am

Forgetting
Mistaking
Hiding
Suppressing
Holding
Ignoring
Mourning

And as I began to unpack my heart
And heal my mind
I grew some wings
And found a new sky
Now I was

Flying
Soaring
Levitating
Exploring
Rising
Ascending
Resurrecting
Freeing
Being

And becoming someone
Who could hug the sun
And kiss the stars
And shake the hand of the moon

Because I had taken
and owned
and protected
and finally reclaimed
my time

rushed fairytale endings

I sing a soft tune
Underneath the mango trees
And hope that one day I'll wake up just as sweet

Deep in my core
hide the seeds I've planted
unknowingly, and sometimes consciously
within my being

I am ripe

I await my next harvest
I know there's something more
I could be

Even as I lie here
Underneath syrupy leaves

But when the sun shines
And nighttime passes. bye
Branches scratch me awake
Maroon dust swirls under my feet
drawing a picture, writing a message
I do not understand

In a surreal state I wonder and wander
half-awake through half-formed dreams
Therein lies the dust of warrior bones

Triumph ensues

Blood spills
Kola nut breaks
And jolted awake
I arise

At a crossroads I find myself
A path obscured stretches ahead
To face fate is a feat
in itself and
I ponder my desires
those thoughts I have abandoned long ago

Still I sprint fast
        Rushing to a finish line

ahead

A daughter is a woman at last
from her feet rise pillars of gold.

Conscious

The pain of black womanhood can feel so politicized to the
point where we subconsciously begin to view ourselves as
abject to our own struggles.
Far removed from the implications
of the pain we experience,
we numb deep wounds with empty kisses
and suffocate under silk scarves
hiding bruised necks.

Vulnerabilities sit at bay, and we duel with the parts of
ourselves
that wish
for a moment,
it would all stop.

I've learned to scream, to shout, and, when all else fails,

to pray.

To cry out my longing to the universe and run to the arms
of God.
She answers my questions with tugs at the hem of my skirt.
She tells me to sit, and wait.
sit, and listen.

sit, and

breathe

Finding comfort in the intricate strands of my being has been
an odyssey inwards:
One of untying strings and looping them through
and coming undone once more.
All to fall through time and space, memory and present,
to find the goddess within me.

She is divine.

And through her I see my own light.
My propensity to birth nations, to steer the head of giants
from calamity, to nurture the seeds of promised lands,
to harvest the fruit of my labor,
of my pain.
Knowing her is knowing my own strength,
the strength that lies in the tapestry of my roots.
Woven with intention and desire

I am divine.

WIND

———

that which carries us

Wind is powerful in the way it transports us
to new discoveries and imaginings
of who we can become, what we can do, how we can evolve.
The wind kisses our backs and tells us to take a step
forward,
even when we believe ourselves to be unready to move on.
We must become the wind on our backs
and carry ourselves to that which we desire,
closing our eyes and surrendering
to the motion of the universe.
Releasing control
is how we learn
to fly.

self-love in quarantine

The flitter of love not yet fully discovered
lingers softly in the horizon
could sun and light and that which is good
still exist
and appear to me from deep within an abyss?

I think it might

my dreams locate me on empty evenings
when lavender lights carry me across
skies that glow in my mind

I am becoming
a woman of virtue
clothed in strength
wrapped in love's soft linens

I have fallen back in love with the essence of who I am
days that end in long sighs beneath a warm Georgia sun

Once I accepted I am destined for greatness
I felt my soul spiral into unknown proportions
I flailed around,
            tumbling,
                    arms flying
which way and that

And as I became
familiar
with the newer dimensions of my narrative
The leaps that fell short
and gates that locked before my grasping hands
fostered the swelling of my heart

First from fear
then from a love awakened

Showing me there is more to me
than I thought I knew

loving me

loving me
is listening to Coltrane
Naima hums so sweetly
and tells me softly
       sugar don't cry
as the windows open waltzing
wildly to soft rain's sweet serenade
the shutters shake in rhythm
so I can feel the sun's bright shine

loving me
is too many cups of green tea
maybe chamomile
sometimes wine
just lying in the moonlight
and losing track of time

loving me
is believing God's promises
Her vision for my life
never doubting Her favor
and knowing I am divine

A Liberated Heart

I am just about ready to hold you tenderly
No longer afraid of shattered glass
And rough pebbles
That mercilessly trip me up along the way
I think it is nearly time I open my palm
Just a moving configuration of lines
The woven fabric of warm flesh
It is nearly time to hold your heart in my hand
To hold you close, my dear,

But I am afraid that my fears have grown wings
Webbed together at night
And they float through my mind each time I begin to
believe it is time

I couldn't imagine what loving could feel like

I could not find it in the iris pools of confusion
you locked me in
Tied up in a bind
I couldn't find love in your eyes
I could only taste it on your lips, sometimes
Only behind closed doors
But never in the light
I could never see your smile clearly
Just a glimpse of flesh, so discreetly

I couldn't imagine what loving could feel like
until I started loving you

I've only just begun to sink my teeth into
Tender figments of my imagination
That once seemed so far
But now hold me close in the thick wool
Of your affections
The intentions of amorous embrace

I've only just begun to taste the cotton candy pillows of care
I drift peacefully
You submerge me in compassionate waters
I happily drown
Succumbing to thoughts unheard
Bliss unseen
Why did we hesitate before
Hidden in fear
Why did you hide from me?

I've only just begun to love
I couldn't imagine what loving could feel like
until I began to love you now

Freely

like morning dew

falling for you
feels so new
the first leap from a racing cloud
and familiar at the same time
the constant kiss of the wind on my neck

our touches are a glimpse into a future
soft
like the mist of a dew predicting
a day when you're mine
if my heart continues to tumble
I hope I pile softly into your arms
awakened by the heights you carry me to

I am falling for you
it feels so new
and familiar at the same time

our touches are a glimpse into a future
your love a low-hanging fruit
ripe with the promise of forever
I feel the draft of new beginnings
soft like the mist of a dew predicting
a day when you're mine

I am falling for you
pulling back the arrow
piercing through my open heart

it feels so new
and familiar at the same time

I am falling for you
boldly
I sink my teeth into your sweet nothings
savoring every bite
I feel the draft of new beginnings

today, I know

you're mine

isn't it euphoric

the rhythmic lulls of your voice
insinuate more to come

the ebb and flow
of our conversations
rush through me like
songbirds flying north

soaring through
starry nights with you
it fills me with bliss
and leads me to question
a life without

this

this meaning you
and you bringing me

through seasonal temperaments
and spring's intoxicating haze
the roundabout park
of looking into your eyes

over and over again
on this carousel you wind me up
surpassing time and space

you lift me higher
to a point of ecstasy

les reves d'amour

falling asleep to the taste of your lips
is the lightness of honeysuckle
savored on a summer day
and your eyes are the stained glass
of opaque windows
that envelop me in merciless delight

your body: the chrysanthemum greens
of a meadow
I could meander through
with eternity on my mind

as nighttime falls and moonlight
holds you near
I can't help but indulge with haste
my kisses climb you slowly,
leisurely, I graze
through your meridian's arc

and as your eyelids flutter to a close
your mind retreating to a world
of your own
I will myself into your dreams

hoping you think of me
like I think of you

A love across seasons

The greys of the clouds
And the light that peeks out
The golden rays
Arrows from Zeus

They all ask me questions
Sending thoughts a flurry
while pensive days become weeks

As the greys turn to reflect
grasses greens
And the naked trees beget
fallen leaves

Scarlet evenings drenched in red wine
drown in sapphire lakes the color of the winter sky

For this, love sings a song
Demeter's soft prelude
To my heart in full bloom

I hope my cherry kisses
Find their way to you

And the world keeps turning

My saving grace is the manner with which I romanticize
every minuscule aspect
of this blessing we call life
Before my soul transcends over this unpredictable arc
into dimensions unknown
I have to pause each day
sometimes to relish
the smell of rain that slowly approaches
at times to hear the melody of children laughing
on the playground while I sit on a nearby bench
and reminisce of a time I was free to run and fall
without the worries of adulthood plaguing my mind
I still like to roll a j and look up at the night sky
it is hard to feel small when I look at the stars
or the jolting glow of a full moon
some feel intimidated by the wonders of this earth
but I love to feel them in my bones
and honor the parts of my body that grow
from earth's vines
I like to imagine my anxious bow of sweat
as a sweet nectar
pulsating through living fruit
I am sweet and ripe with dreams and ideas for how to enjoy
my time here fully
and as I look at trees
and say hi to leaves
and smell flowers that die and come back to life
I feel full to the brim
with gratitude for an earth that kisses me goodnight
and hugs me good morning

she doesn't have to do so
but should my body decompose into her soils one day
I know she will keep my spirit alive through happy leaves
and singing bees
humming about
spreading my sweet nectar around
and around

idle thoughts

dawn suffocates me
in those early hours
when my dreams and fears intertwine
they morph into a deceptive smile
that taunts me with uncertainty
of a future I have not yet tasted

I'm in the mood for better
I have appetite for more
beyond the fixations I hold dear
it is hope that silences doubt
when the two collide
at the vapid shores of my idle discontent

if there is a shadow being
hiding in the dark
come out and reveal your ways
so I may never hide my thoughts again
in a canister of solitude
and hesitations that linger for too long
momentarily in the way

my fears waltz in tune
until they fall from risen clouds
in the soft fog of this silent hour

I can reach for those higher dreams
and claim them

as my own

art

I move my hand in rhythm with my heart
and sketch an ocean of dreams
lost in a whirlpool of reality
sunken in the depths of what was last night
but is not
today

I paint a desert of fears
splattered with dry skulls of disbelief
an oasis of courage graces the corners
in a desperate attempt to expand
it falters to the wayside
but is saved by faith's quick hand

I draw a sky of love
where hearts beat and rise
in exquisite harmony
flapping their wings into heaven
and joining the angels in beautiful symphony
of compassion's glowing light

I write a world of serenity
Birds mimic gazelles in the air
smiles rest in abundance
and laughter glides through souls
as we toast to the pulsating rhythms of our hearts

Palm leaves shiver in the wind
I dance by the sea
thunder spells out a sonnet in the sky
sparrows sing to me as I go about my day

I breathe
you do the same

When I hesitate at heaven's gates
fear threatening to taint
the sun pens a letter in the clouds
asking me one question
carried through wind's song

      are you not art?

a creation
limbs glued, crafted
by a masterful being who with intention
masters your existence
into a light
so powerful
one can only call it
life

dynamic
impassioned
whole

      alive

where I came from

How black was your childhood?

I never knew until Brown catapulted me into an ivory sea
surrounded by people who were searching
for that sense of camaraderie in strangers
united mostly by skin color
class and life experiences aside
It never occurred to me to put a litmus test to my identity

When hands were smaller and laughter more free
we used to go to the tree on the far side of the playground
and pick honeysuckle to suck the sweetness
Then we would practice singing our runs
memorizing lyrics from Writings on the Wall
and taking in breaths to belt
like a young Keyshia Cole

We spent summers at the community pool
with our play cousins who always dared me to jump
into the deep end
but I wasn't ready

Movie nights at Stonecrest were fun
when my older sister was in town
because then we could buy all the pop-tarts we wanted
from the Target across the street
and hide them in her purse
without anyone suspecting a thing

How black was your childhood?

Coach Davis was my favorite gym teacher
because he would always rap
"Welcome to Atlanta where the players play"
whenever we had a new kid in class
Oh! and I can't forget learning how to make
the perfect mac 'n' cheese
from Miss Peco's recipe
because her sweet potato pie gave me life
in ways only a meal prepared with love could do

If I close my eyes I can hear
my doctor's office playing Cece Winans and Dottie Peoples
in the waiting room
The receptionist gave us stickers whenever we left
and I smiled even when I later found them crumpled up
in the backseat of my mom's car

My favorite teacher was an AKA
so I wanted to wear pink and green too
because I thought Ms. Ferguson was
the epitome of excellence

How black was your childhood?

Fela floated from my dad's record player
on early Saturday mornings
and sometimes we would sing Stevie Wonder
from my favorite CD
followed by Brandy

Every so often my dad would let me sit in the front seat
of his white convertible as we cruised down South Deshon

but never when we went to the Piccadilly
on Memorial Drive
after long Sunday mornings spent at church

Weekend trips to Dekalb Farmers Market
made me happy to be different
because they ended with the sweet aroma
of my mother's egusi soup
and the comfort of knowing she would be there tomorrow

Running through the fountains at Centennial Park
and feeling the rain of summer's sweat fall down my back
I knew that life was meant for living

*So, how ~~black~~, no, **amazing** was my childhood?*

I guess I never realized until now.

letter to my twelve-year-old self

Dear little girl
you tried to carve the pain
out your veins
with a sharpened blade
whose edge went null against
your turbid wounds
invisible to the eye

little girl
you wept raging seas
into a pillow that failed to silence your ache
and left you
lying awake
contemplating a cumbersome fate, you clung to a life raft
built from your mind's imaginings

little girl
you ran from the mirror
that forced you to look
and see what was left
of your soul
the deformities, the promise
the fortitude you struggled to develop
and the tears you had to hide
and the pain you had to hold

it won't be like this forever
little girl
just keep your head up
if you could see the bright horizon

then I promise
love and laughter would raise your sunken ship
from depths of desperation and despair

a promised land awaits you
the mirage of new beginnings
will no longer evade your line of sight
the beauty in the darkness that
caused you to stumble
is that which guides you
towards the light

almost is not your forever
you are infinite beyond even your most limiting beliefs

If I could hold you
and lift you to the clouds
to show you the galaxies you will inherit
and wrap you in the warmth of the sun

you would know good days are coming
you would rest assured in your power
and cognizance of your calling

little girl
just know this
I love you
Wipe your tears my darling
my beautifully crafted divine being
you are an angel walking this earth
your footsteps will rest in the sands of time
forever

your mere existence is a reflection of resilience
beauty, might, and power
my dear
you must always remember
this is your truth

Love,

The future that awaits you

We

the power of she
a steady drum

she leads
beat upon beat
hit yet alive
she succeeds
pushing to thrive

be alive

the power of we
fabric of clouds
we rise
thread upon thread
frayed, never undone
we climb
painting pictures of hope

be alive

we are Funmilayo Kuti, we are Brenda Fassie
we are Lupita Nyong'o,
we are Her Excellency Dr. Joyce Banda,
we are Ama Ata Aidoo, we are Buchi Emecheta,
we are Winnie Mandela, we are Mariama Bâ
We are the revolutionaries of our time

We,
African women,
pillars
mountains
shakers
support and steady
breaking yet standing
building and growing
transcending time space and power to be
we are the futures we sew so faithfully into

vested in us, worlds of hope
imaginings to be

we

Black Girl Magic

What do they mean when they say Black women are magic?

Is it the knowing glances we share in public?
That nod of approval when we see a fellow sister flourishing.
Maybe the glistening of our skin when golden hour hits
just right. Or perhaps it is the manner with which we rise
from ashes, our love's alchemy transforming barren bones
into luscious gardens.
Our wings carry us gently, surpassing eagles
and holding hands
with a sun that begs us to join her each day.

Sometimes, when I am alone
and surrounded by the soft hum of the present,
I think of a past that I was not a part of
and the future that awaits me.

What parts of my ancestors did I inherit?
Am I a walking manifestation of their wildest dreams?
Did their imaginations, their fervent prayers, their
offerings to the Earth conjure me into becoming the
woman I am today?
A mighty oak whose roots extend
beyond the meadows she knows.
A sunflower who looks to the sun, patiently assured
that she will greet her with love each day.
A river that runs against the wind.
Against all odds.

I wonder if every Black woman has had this thought
at some point in her life.
Which Black woman of yore had to turn
lemons into lemonade
in order for me to be here today?

To flow abundantly, at times sour or sweet
—but free all the same.

I Write What I Like

I believe that African women must find our own revolution
And that we must prepare to bear arms for our virtue
and our right to the treasures of this Earth
And I am infatuated with this imagining
of the African woman
free
uninhibited
and daring to be more
more than a
mother
sister
lover
or a pillar standing still
and patiently waiting
to receive

When, in fact, we created love
in all her glory

and our breasts bear Aphrodite's kiss
and our minds move mountains
as our thoughts roar loud
And the thunder shakes to the rhythmic step of our feet
So yes, we are the siren's delight
Singing a song that can break you
and enchant you all the same

The African woman is ethereal
Uniquely bound to a celestial host

the sun
the moons
the stars
our beings are connected
with the land and the sea
and the middle ground where the two kiss and finally meet

So I take this to mean
And, no, I do not say it respectfully
We must sink the ships of pirates
In all their unique forms
And castrate audacious men who try to claim our shores
We must rumble the foundations of those colosseums
in the middle of which we stand
We are no longer servants
This is our Holy Land

I pen this note to my valiant sisters
Those awake and those who sleep
This is a call to action
Please read this carefully

Where oceans rise
Our feet will not fall
Where the earth crumbles
We will stand tall
Where cries break glass
And fires rage on
We will conquer calamities
and the crack of lightning's whip

may I remind you
the lineage from which we come
We are the span of evolving moons
The infinite range of stars

And lest you forget our power

We are the fortitude that burns

incessantly
with the raging sun

Force of Nature

I laugh in the face of men
who grab at air and fail
falling flat
beneath me

I am not a feminist
I am a revolutionary

I tip tap, waltzing
Tip toeing, never

Always gliding

To the promise land
That which is

Free.

Above all things

And flowing with milk and honey
Into the soft curves of my breasts
Deep valleys that feed into a mystifying maze

My forefathers danced on a compound sprinkled with the
blood of the colonizer
and sang tribute to the sunken ships
of comrades long gone

Because sometimes war means light
shining through the hurricane's eye
Because many times change means tears
that evaporate from buoyant seas
sitting untouched
And new beginnings and unlearning and erasing
And starting all over and becoming

Light.

Daisies sprout from the crown of my head
Because light is in my smile
And the soft coil of my hair
And the smell of coconut oil glistening
under a sky the color of gold
Illuminating all that I am
and all that is in me
Reminding the earth's soil
that once upon a time we were

One.

Until I was formed within God's unique mold
Shaped with gentle hands
under the meticulous care
of a benign potter's gaze
The maker of earth's clay

Curator of delicacies that stretch through
mountainous heights
and flow through
treacherous ravines
collecting peacefully
at an oasis end

Gazelles graze at the pastures of my hips
powerful oaks rise from the depths of my womb
The melodies of leaves that whisper to me
remind me that
I am

a force of nature

ACKNOWLEDGEMENTS

———

This book is an ode to the beauty of love, growth, and community. It was a long and arduous road to get here, and I could not have done so alone.

I am able to present *Force of Nature* to the world because I had the love of my community to nourish my soul and carry me forward. I am filled with the deepest gratitude for every single person who has made me feel safe enough to share such an intimate piece of myself with the world. May God bless you as you have blessed me.

Thank you first and foremost to my family for loving me and supporting me every time I came up with a new goal. You never make me feel crazy for dreaming. My love for you is immeasurable. Thank you to my older sister, Linda, for always believing in me and challenging me to think about life from a perspective different from my own. You inspire me more than you know. Thank you to my younger sister, Toju, for listening to my random musings and giving me feedback on my poems. Oh, and thank you for the TikTok videos that made me smile when I was super stressed with revisions. You make me happy to be a big sister. Thank you to my ancestors; you dreamed the freedom I now experience and imagined the galaxies I will inherit. Thank you for your existence and your angelic guiding light.

Thank you to the most important men in my life who helped me become the woman I am today—my father, Uncle Pierre, and Uncle Lanre. Thank you for your love and constant encouragement. Thank you to my grandfather; your life is an inspiration and reminder of the prowess ingrained within our lineage.

Thank you to my dearest friends who see me, truly, for who I am. Akosua, Naomi, Peter, Nasar, Dolapo, Josie, Sophia, Dawn, Maryam—thank you for being a source of light in my life. You have all impacted me deeply and have loved me even when I didn't always show love towards myself. Thank you for teaching me the power of unconditional love.

Thank you to Aunty Mo and Aunty Shetu for reminding me that self-love is the greatest love of all! I love you both with all my heart; you both remind me that there is strength in being true to yourself, no matter what tradition or society tells us. You show me that it is okay to start over and redefine womanhood on my own terms.

Thank you to my amazing beta readers, Seya and Haley. Your thoughtful feedback gave me the confidence I needed to push through to the end of my revisions process.

Thank you to the educators who have helped me see the world through lenses of curiosity and wonder. You helped me hone the power of my words and taught me how to use the power of knowledge to change the world. Mrs. Brouillard, Mrs. Ferguson, Ms. Malloy, Mr. Young, Don Donelson, Professor Agupusi, and Anani, who is gone too soon, but will forever be in my heart—thank you.

Thank you to my mentor, Mr. Mallory, for believing in me and always answering the phone when I need life advice.

Thank you, Professor Eric Koester. You took a chance on a writer trying to be heard in a major way and the Creator Institute helped make this dream a reality.

Thank you to every single person who pre-ordered my book; your support carried me to the finish line. Thank you:

Bomo Opigo Pessu, Linda Sooh, Toju Pessu, Noghor Pessu, Emi Daria , Alexandra DeFrancesco Devin Gray, Haley Gray, Terricia Soyombo, Olugbade Alli, JoNella Queen, Sophia Danner-Okotie, Jonathan Famery, Jimmy Stone, Trent Nkomo, Jalencia Wade, Rosemary Astra-Blossom, Paula Jaja, Ameyo Attila, Grace Larson, Sarah Olushoga, Faridah A Koledoye, Adesola Sanusi, Nony Odim, Neil Thakral, Dami Saliu, Eniola Aina, Damisola Balogun, Barrett Hazeltine, Chelsea Gray, Julian Medina, Tamarah Costen, Tobi Soyebo, Leticia Calvillo, Joanna Massa, Eyimofe Pessu, Martine Jean-Charles, Alexandra Chukwumah, Fadwa Ahmed, Seya Lewis-Meeks, Peter Clarke, Kwadwo A. Yeboah-Kankam, Ramita Ravi, Uzoamaka Okoro,David Leziga Manadom, Chichi Agbim, Christopher Brock, Allbertrand Pierre, Kana Hamamoto, Eric Baffour, Toby Okwara, Maryam Bagudu, Nivita Chaliki, Yansy Salmeron,Francis Rosenberg, Mark Lee, Connor Gregory, Sam

Lin-Sommer, Paul Touma, Reid Shea, Joshua Daniel, Koya Olateru, Kiran Cartolari, Carly Paul, James Archer, Kaye Lin Kuphal, Peace Jaja, Jacob Mukand, Jake Miller, Charles Dike, Lanre Omonaiye, Jessica Thigpen, Josh Gelberger, Lucas P. Johnson, Dawn Awonaike, Edi Umoren, Deanna Devonshuk, Stephen Okala, Blessing Ubani, Christine Kong, Alissa Rhee, Don Donelson, Drew Solomon, Abigail Neill, Eliza Robertson, Peter Matthew Simpson, Jordan A Evans, Eric Koester, Herbert Spurlock III, Selwyn Walker, Kwaku Kankam, Jr., Anica Green, Morgan Paige, Brandon Burke, Yacine Sow, Olugbenga Joseph, Dylynne Dodson, AynNichelle Slappy, Tonita Washington, Alexandra Curtis, Dolapo Akinkugbe, Aimee Okotie-Oyekan, Stella Mensah, Folashade Adeyemo, Gregory Stewart, Ava Raddatz, Roli Ibadin, LaVoisia Michele Jones, Akosua Bekoe, Maureen Legemah, Chioma Nnamdi-Emetarom, Jude Mmereole, Faith Wright, Nasar Dike, Mallet Njonkem, Ada Agbim, Richard Legemah, Tuebi Zuofa, Ola Awonaike, Amishetu Mabiaku, Andy Okala, Kennedy Gibson-Wynn, Constance Gamache, Sarah Yoho, Linda Wendy Medina, Modupe Kusimo, Stanton L Geyer, Paul B Muah, Danielle Badaki, Richard Jarvis III, Ayesha Harisinghani, Shauna Tulloch, Jeanine Mason, Christopher Calley, Angie Cruz, Jacqueline Agustin, Afua Osei, Sophia Kiang, Cristina Taylor, Naomi Kouassi, Rakan Aboneaaj, Jada Banks.

And—last but not least! To my dear readers, thank you for embarking on this journey with me. I invite you to continue voyaging into the depths of your soul to discover who you are truly meant to be. Spend time with yourself, speak to yourself kindly, and never ever forget what an immense force of nature you are. Go and take this life by storm; the world is yours.

Made in the USA
Columbia, SC
20 June 2021

39909509R00095